THE KREGEL PICTORIAL GUIDE TO THE TEMPLE

ROBERT BACKHOUSE

EDITED BY DR TIM DOWLEY

The great doors of Herod's Temple, from Alec Garrard's authentic model.

kregel
PUBLICATIONS

Grand Rapids, MI 49501

**Library of Congress
Cataloging-in-Publication Data**

Backhouse, Robert.
  The Kregel pictorial guide to the Temple /
Robert Backhouse.
    p. cm.
  Includes index.
  1. Temple of Jerusalem (Jerusalem)—History.
2. Tabernacle. I. Title.
BM655.B33   1996   296.4—dc20
                                        96-10725
ISBN 0-8254-3039-9   CIP

  6 7 8 9 10 11 12 / 08 07 06 05 04 03 02
        Printed in Singapore

Mr. Alec Garrard of Fressingfield, Norfolk, England, is the builder of the magnificent temple model featured in this book. His authentic model is based on information from the Bible, the Talmud, the Mishnah, Flavius Josephus, Alfred Edersheim, F. W. Farrar, and the latest archaeological discoveries. Built to a scale of 1:100, each handmade "brick" was baked in the family oven. Mr. Garrard, a Norfolk farmer, former builder, and lay preacher, constructed this labor of a lifetime in a barn adjacent to his sixteenth-century farmhouse at Moat Farm.

(Photographs in this book may not be reproduced without the written permission of Angus Hudson, Ltd.)

Published by Kregel Publications, a division of Kregel, Inc.,
P. O. Box 2607, Grand Rapids, MI 49501.

Designed and created by Three's Company
5 Dryden Street, London WC2E 9NW

Additional Works from Kregel Publications

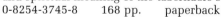
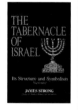

kregel
PUBLICATIONS

www.kregel.com

Contents

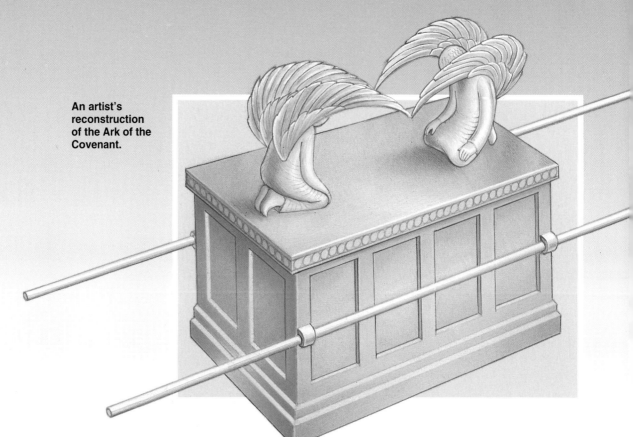

An artist's reconstruction of the Ark of the Covenant.

An artist's impression of sacrifices at the Tabernacle. In the foreground a priest is blowing on a ram's horn trumpet.

The Tabernacle

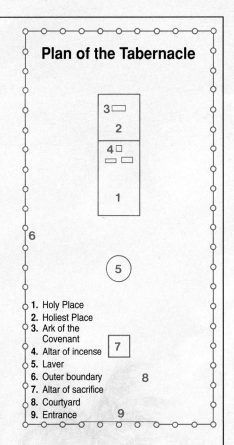

Plan of the Tabernacle

1. Holy Place
2. Holiest Place
3. Ark of the Covenant
4. Altar of incense
5. Laver
6. Outer boundary
7. Altar of sacrifice
8. Courtyard
9. Entrance

The Tabernacle, or Tent of Meeting, was first set up at Mount Sinai by the Israelites after their escape from slavery in Egypt. Through it God taught them how they were to worship him. When Moses entered the tent, 'the LORD would speak to Moses face to face as a man speaks to his friend' (Exodus 33:11).

Construction

The outer boundary of the Tabernacle area was made up of curtains hung over a metal framework, and measured 46 metres (150 ft) by 23 metres (75 feet), and 2.3 metres (7 feet 6 inches) high.

The Tabernacle itself was a large tent measuring 13.7 x 4.6 metres (45 x 15 feet). The idea of 'God's tent', a portable structure, was specially suitable for the Israelites as they travelled through the Wilderness. It had two rooms: an outer room, the Holy Place, where only priests were allowed; and an inner room, called the Holiest Place, or Holy of Holies, only entered once a year by the high priest. Here stood the Ark of the Covenant, containing the Ten Commandments and other precious things.

Outside in the courtyard stood the altar on which sacrifices of goats, lambs, bulls and other animals were burnt, and a bronze washing basin, or laver.

At the Tabernacle God's people met with the presence of God.

An artist's impression of Solomon's Temple, with the great laver, or bronze ritual washing basin. The capitals of the pillars on either side of the Temple doorway were each decorated with 200 pomegranates.

Solomon's Temple

King David was not permitted to build a Temple, though he collected money and materials for its construction. His son, Solomon, took seven years to build the first Temple in Jerusalem. It was twice the size of the portable Tabernacle which it replaced and on which it was modelled. (The Tabernacle had been brought to Jerusalem: 1 Kings 8:1-5.)

Solomon used the forced labour of 80,000 quarrymen and 70,000 porters to cut and transport huge stones for building the Temple; and 30,000 Israelites collected cedar and juniper wood from Lebanon. The Temple was panelled with cedar, on which

skilled Phoenician craftsmen carved cherubim, flowers and palm trees, before the whole interior was overlaid in gold.

Outside the Temple stood a three-tiered bronze altar and a great bronze basin (the laver) for ritual washing, supported by twelve bronze oxen, three at each point of the compass.

The double doors of cypress wood, which opened into the Holy Place, were flanked by two pillars, on the right Jachin, and on the left Boaz.

Solomon's Temple, a fulfilment of King David's dream, was a monument to the glory of God (see 1 Kings 6-7; 2 Chronicles 3-4).

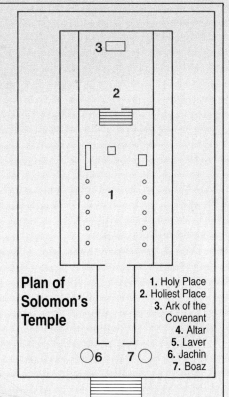

Plan of Solomon's Temple

1. Holy Place
2. Holiest Place
3. Ark of the Covenant
4. Altar
5. Laver
6. Jachin
7. Boaz

Solomon to Herod

Jewish shekel (AD 132-135) depicting Herod's Temple.

From Solomon to Herod

Solomon's splendid Temple had a checkered history of neglect, plunder (King Shishak of Egypt captured some of its treasures during the reign of Solomon's son, Rehoboam), misuse (King Manasseh reintroduced pagan practices and 'built altars to all the starry hosts' – 2 Kings 21:4-5) and looting and destruction under the Assyrian King Nebuchadrezzar in 587 BC. The Ark of the Covenant disappeared at the time of the exile, and was never recovered or replaced.

Under the leadership of King Zerubbabel and the High Priest Joshua, the Israelites rebuilt Solomon's Temple, but on a far inferior scale. When the foundation stone of this Temple was laid, many of 'the older priests wept aloud' in disappointment (Ezra 3:7-13).

The prophets of the Old Testament encouraged the returned Jewish exiles to complete the restoration of the Temple and worship God faithfully there. The prophet Haggai asked pointedly, 'Is it a time for you yourselves to be living in your panelled houses, while this house [the Temple] remains a ruin?' (Haggai 1:4).

The Second Temple was probably improved and more elaborately adorned during the third and second centuries BC, but we know little about this period in its history. On December 15 167 BC Antiochus IV, the Seleucid king, set up a pagan altar in the Temple, thereby ritually polluting it for the Jews. When the Jewish heroes the Maccabees defeated the Seleucids, they had to cleanse the Temple and rededicate it (1 Maccabees 4:36-59). In 63 BC the Roman general Pompey captured Jerusalem.

A political move

King Herod now rebuilt the Temple. Herod, King of Judea 37 BC-AD 4, was not a Jew by birth, but a descendant of the hated Edomites, and a member of the Idumean dynasty. An outsider, he was also loathed by the Jews for killing some of the rival Jewish Hasmonean family, and for having a Samaritan, Malthace, among his ten wives.

Magnificent

While Herod's Temple was unquestionably the largest and most magnificent of the three temples, it was not built by him for the glory of God, but to curry favour with the Jews, whom he had to keep in order if he wanted to remain a puppet king within the Roman Empire.

Herod the Great

Herodium

Herod loved grandiose building projects. The Herodium ranks as one of the largest fortresses ever built for the protection of one man, and as the greatest engineering feat yet discovered in the inter-testamental period. Built on top of a huge cone-shaped mount 11 kilometres (seven miles) south of Jerusalem, with four towers (three semi-circular, and one rounded), it was protected by an outer double wall with a three metre (10 foot) passageway between the walls.

When Jerusalem was destroyed in AD 70, the Herodium was one of three major sites of Jewish resistance outside Jerusalem. The second century Jewish Bar Kokhba Revolt also used the Herodium as its headquarters.

Masada

Masada, Herod's other palace fortress, was located on the western shore of the Dead Sea, and served as his summer resort. This virtually impregnable bolt-hole was lavishly furnished, as the excavated bath-house and storerooms have revealed.

Fanatical Jewish zealots made their last stand against Rome in AD 73 at Masada. Rather than be captured by the Romans, they entered into a suicide pact, first killing their wives and children and then themselves.

The remains of Herod's northern palace in profile at Masada.

Jerusalem in AD 30

God's city
This artist's impression of the city of Jerusalem in Jesus' day shows Herod's Temple, the greatest of Herod's building enterprises, which he started in 19 BC and which covered over 15 percent of the total area of Jerusalem.

Jerusalem is one of the world's great cities, and is a holy city for three religions, Christianity, Judaism and Islam. In the Jewish religion and in Christian teaching, Jerusalem is God's city. It was the most important city in Israel's history.

In Jesus' day, Jerusalem was the center for Jewish faith and worship. It was also the setting for the last week of Jesus' life, and for the most momentous events in God's plan of salvation.

Jesus spoke to his disciples about Jerusalem: 'We are going up to Jerusalem, and everything that is written by the prophets about the Son of Man will be fulfilled. He will be turned over to

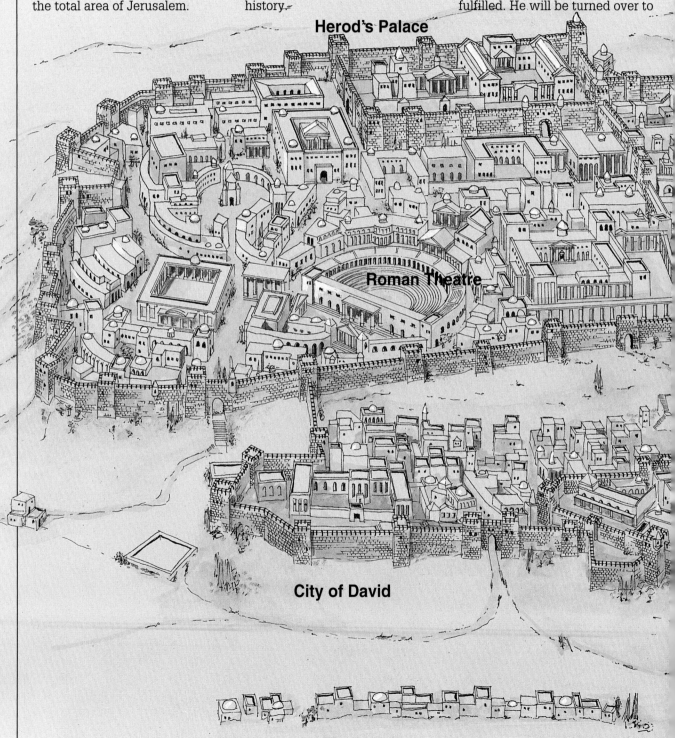

Herod's Palace

Roman Theatre

City of David

the Gentiles. They will mock him, insult him, spit on him, flog him and kill him. On the third day he will rise again' (Luke 18:31-33).

Jesus revealed his great love for Jerusalem when he said, 'O Jerusalem, Jerusalem, you who kill the prophets and stone those sent to you, how often I have longed to gather your children together, as a hen gathers her chicks under her wings, but you

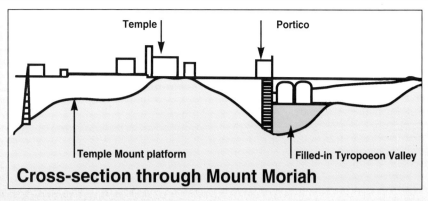

Cross-section through Mount Moriah

were not willing. Look, your house is left to you desolate' (Matthew 23:37-38).

Here, as a baby, Jesus was 'presented' (Luke 2:22), and from its courts Jesus later witnessed the poor widow 'casting her two mites into the treasury' (Luke 21:1-4).

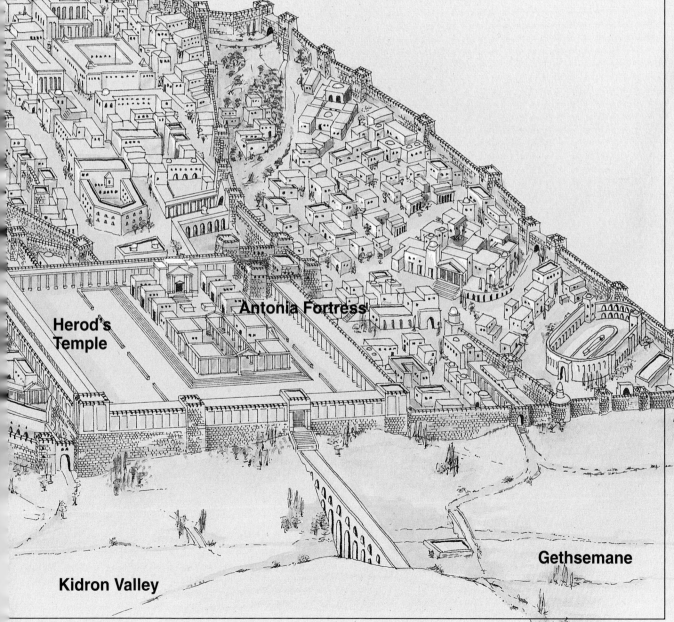

Golgotha

Herod's Temple

Antonia Fortress

Gethsemane

Kidron Valley

Herod Builds a Temple

Herod the Great undertook a massive building program in Jerusalem. An area of about 15 hectares (36 acres) was enclosed by a massive wall around the top of the hill on which the city stood, the hollow areas were filled with rubble, or made into crypts used for storage or stabling. The surrounding wall measured about 305 metres (1,000 feet) in length and originally enclosed King Solomon's Palace, at the southern end, and was at a lower level than the Temple platform. When King Herod enlarged and beautified the Temple, the entire platform was raised to the higher level. Herod began work on the Temple in 19 BC, and finished the Sanctuary in 12 BC. But the building work was not finally completed until AD 64.

The pattern of worship
Worship in the Temple was based on that of the Tabernacle, only everything was on a far grander scale. Around the east-facing Temple a series of courts was set aside for different purposes.

A wall about 1.5 metres (4 feet six inches) high called 'the Wall of Partition' surrounded the Sanctuary, and beyond this wall none but a Jew could pass, on

pain of death. A notice to this effect was discovered in Jerusalem in 1871 engraved on a block of limestone 57 x 85 cm (22 x 33 inches). It reads: '*No stranger is to enter within the balustrade around the temple and enclosure: whoever is caught will be responsible to himself for his death, which will ensue*' (see Acts 21:26ff; Ephesians 2:14-18).

Passing within the Wall of Partition, a flight of 12 steps led up to an area 3 metres (9 feet) higher, where the Women's Gate and Gate of the the Pure and Just gave access to a paved court known as the Court of Prayer.

At the end of this court, on a semi-circular raised dais, sacrifices and gifts were brought to be presented to the Lord.

Beyond this was the Court of Priests, with its great altar of sacrifice and brazen laver for the ceremonial washing of priests. The porch led into the Sanctuary itself, comprising the Holy Place and the Holiest Place.

Inscription barring non-Jews from the sanctified area of the Temple.

Inside the Sanctuary
Inside the Holy Place were the seven-branched golden lampstand, the table of showbread and the altar of incense. The Holiest Place was about 9 x 9 metres (30 feet square) and 18 metres (60 feet) high, and separated from the Holy Place by a great curtain (see Luke 23:45).

Plan of the Temple

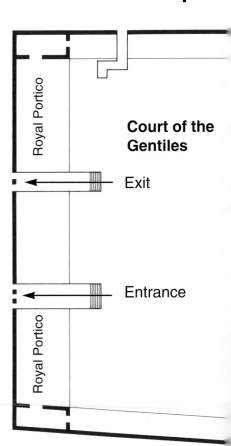

Royal Portico

Court of the Gentiles

Exit

Entrance

Royal Portico

The south-west corner of the wall around the Temple Mount, with 'Robinson's Arch', the remains of a broad arch connecting the city with the Temple.

The Antonia Fortress

Herod named his Antonia Fortress after Mark Antony, the friend of Julius Caesar. After Antony defeated Caesar's enemies in northern Greece, he appointed Herod as tetrarch (ruler of a fourth) of Galilee (see Matthew 14:1). The Roman military tribune, who acted as chief of police, was stationed with his men in the Antonia Fortress, which also guarded Herod's Temple.

This great fortress at the north-west corner of the Temple area is where the apostle Paul was imprisoned for his own safety when the Jewish leaders plotted to take his life (Acts 22).

Alec Garrard's model of the Antonia Fortress, named after Mark Antony.

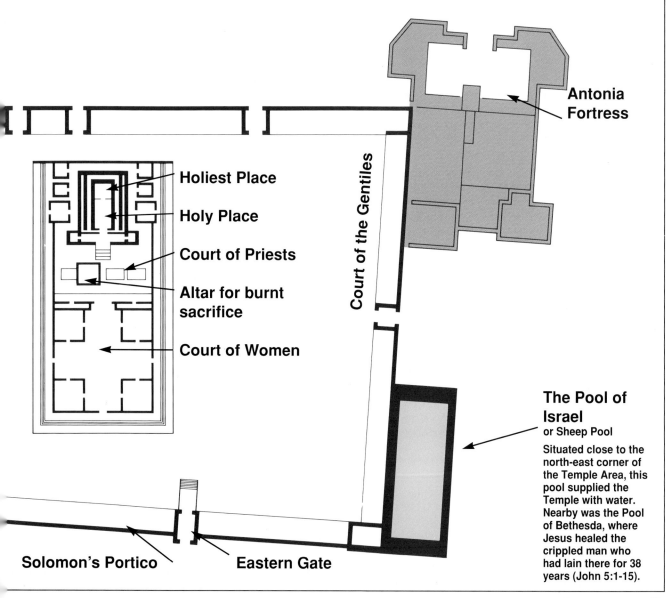

Holiest Place

Holy Place

Court of Priests

Altar for burnt sacrifice

Court of Women

Court of the Gentiles

Antonia Fortress

The Pool of Israel
or Sheep Pool

Situated close to the north-east corner of the Temple Area, this pool supplied the Temple with water. Nearby was the Pool of Bethesda, where Jesus healed the crippled man who had lain there for 38 years (John 5:1-15).

Solomon's Portico

Eastern Gate

13

Temple Rituals

The High Priest was the central human figure in the drama of the sacrificial ritual. He wore symbolic clothes, such as the breastplate strapped over his chest which held twelve precious stones, each engraved with the name of one of the twelve tribes of Israel. In the top row were ruby, topaz and carbuncle; in the second row, turquoise, sapphire and emerald; in the third row, jacinth, agate and amethyst; and in the bottom row, chrysalite, onyx and jasper (Exodus 39:8-21).

The main duty of the Temple priests was to offer daily animal sacrifices on behalf of the people.

Only the High Priest was allowed into the Holiest Place, only once a year, on the Day of Atonement (*Yom Kippur*), when he sprinkled the blood of two sacrificed animals on the cover of the Ark of the Covenant, the place where, symbolically, God met his people (Leviticus 16).

Aaron, the first high priest, is pictured putting blood from a slaughtered calf on the horns of the altar, as a sin offering (see Leviticus 9:8-11).

Old Testament sacrifices

The five sacrifices made in Old Testament times were:

1. Burnt offering, when a bull (dove for the poor) was offered as an act of worship.

2. Sin offering, when a bull or goat (dove for the poor) was offered for the forgiveness of sins.

3. Grain offering, when baked bread was offered to recognize God's provision.

4. Fellowship offering, when a perfect animal was offered in thanksgiving.

5. Guilt offering, when a ram or lamb was offered to make restitution for sin (Leviticus 5).

In the New Testament the book of Hebrews takes up this language about sacrifices, calling Christ our high priest, and declaring, 'we have been made holy through the sacrifice of the body of Jesus Christ once for all' (Hebrews 10:10). The writer stresses that 'without the shedding of blood there is no forgiveness' (Hebrews 9:22).

Above: The Sheep Pool, outside the Temple, where animals were washed.
Below: The sheep and cattle pens, where animals were kept for sacrifice.

Below: The tradesmen's stall outside the Temple, as shown on Mr Garrard's scale model.

This overall view of the Temple constructed by Mr Alec Garrard gives a fine impression of the monumental scale of the structure and of the extensive surrounding courts.

Herod's Temple

Herod's magnificent 50 meter (150 feet) high structure greatly impressed the disciple who said to Jesus, 'Look, Teacher! What massive stones! What magnificent buildings!' Jesus replied, 'Not one stone here will be left on another; every one will be thrown down' (Mark 13:1-2).

Jesus also used the Temple to illustrate his resurrection, when he said, 'Destroy this temple, and I will raise it again in three days.' The Jews protested, 'It has taken forty-six years to build this temple.' John explains, 'But the temple he had spoken of was his body' (John 2:18-21).

The Altar of Sacrifice

Priests prepared the animals for sacrifice on the altar in the Court of the Priests. The sacrificial system was so familiar to the Jews that John the Baptist's first recorded words about Jesus would have needed no explanation: 'Look, the Lamb of God, who takes away the sin of the world!' (John 1:29).

Temple Festivals

God gave the Jewish people numerous feast days, or festivals, to celebrate different events through the year. The Feast of Passover, the Feast of Pentecost and the Feast of Tabernacles were the three major festivals.

Feast of Pentecost

The Feast of Pentecost (Harvest, or Weeks) was to give thanks for the Lord's blessing on the harvest. Two leavened wave loaves were offered, and two one-year-old lambs sacrificed as wave offerings – given to God and received back (Leviticus 23:15-22).

Feast of Tabernacles

During the Feast of Tabernacles (Booths, or Ingathering), a week-long celebration for the harvest, the Jews lived in make-shift shelters of branches (booths) to commemorate the Hebrews' journey from Egypt to Canaan, and to thank God for the rich produce of Canaan. The Jews had to take 'choice fruits from the trees, and palm fronds, leafy branches and poplars and rejoice before the LORD your God for seven days' (Leviticus 23:33-40).

In the Temple 70 bullocks were offered, in sacrifice for the 70 nations of the world. Each day the Law was read, the Temple trumpets sounded a 21-trumpet fanfare and the ritual of 'drawing water' was acted out. A priest went with a golden water jug to the Pool of Siloam and solemnly drew out three 'logs' of water. To the accompaniment of the Temple trumpets the water was carried to the top of the altar slope and

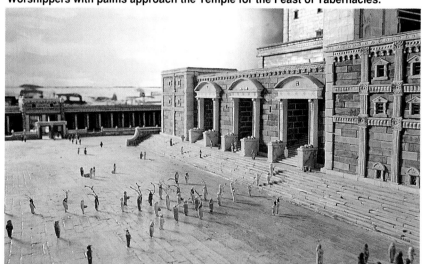

Worshippers with palms approach the Temple for the Feast of Tabernacles.

The red heifer is led outside the Temple precincts on the Day of Atonement, to be burnt on the Mount of Olives.

A seven-branched lampstand.

poured into a silver basin on the western side. Jesus, aware of the spiritual longings of the crowd in the Temple said on the last day of the great festival, 'If any one is thirsty let him come to me and drink' (John 7:37).

Day of Atonement (*Yom Kippur*)

The day of national confession, when the High Priest went into the Holiest Place of the Temple to sprinkle blood of the sacrifice (Leviticus 23:26-32).

New moon

The Jews celebrated the beginning of each month as they had been commanded (Numbers 28:11).

Feast of Firstfruits

During this festival a sheaf of the first barley was presented as a wave offering, and a burnt offering and grain offering were made (Leviticus 23:9-14).

Feast of Trumpets

This festival, later known as *Rosh Hashanah* – New Year's Day, remembered when the Lord said to Moses, 'you are to have a day of rest, a sacred assembly commemorated with trumpet blasts' (see Leviticus 23:23-25).

Feast of Passover

The Feast of Passover (*Pesach*) celebrated Israel's deliverance from slavery in Egypt, and the angel of death's passing over the Israelite children. This feast started with each Jewish family eating their own Passover meal (*Seder*) in their own homes, in symbolic re-enactment of the first Passover. It was held in April (Nisan 14). This was the meal Jesus ate with his disciples in the Upper Room in Jerusalem on the day we now call Maundy Thursday.

Feast of Unleavened Bread

A further seven days of holiday, the Feast of Unleavened Bread, followed Passover, during which Jewish families ate unleavened bread, as they remembered the 40 years they had wandered in the Wilderness. The Jews were told, 'Present to the LORD an offering made by fire, a burnt offering of two young bulls, one ram and seven male lambs a year old, all without defect. With each bull prepare a grain offering of three-tenths of an ephah of fine flour mixed with oil . . . Include one male goat as a sin offering to make atonement for you' (Numbers 28:19-21).

A traditional plate containing the symbolic foods eaten at the Passover meal.

Unleavened Bread on a reconstruction of the Table of Showbread.

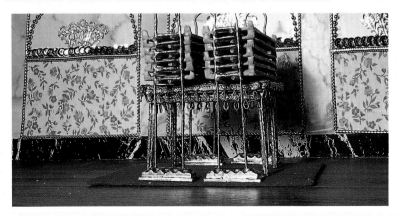

Jesus and the Temple

Jesus 'lost' in Jerusalem

The only incident about Jesus' boyhood recorded in the Gospels revolves around the Temple (see Luke 2:41-52). At the age of twelve, Jesus went with Mary and Joseph to Jerusalem for the Feast of the Passover. (The Law did not say that women should go to the Temple, but Mary gladly obeyed the recommendation of Rabbi Hillel, and accompanied her husband each year – on this occasion they took Jesus too.)

Twelve was a milestone in the life of a Jewish boy. Now he had to start learning a trade to support himself and became 'a son of the Law'.

After the feast, Jesus stayed on in Jerusalem. Mary and Joseph thought Jesus was in their party travelling home to Nazareth. When they could not find him in their group, they returned to Jerusalem to look for him.

After three days, they found Jesus in the Temple courts, sitting among the teachers (where usually only learned rabbis – experts in Judaism – were allowed), listening and asking them questions. 'Everyone who heard him was amazed at his understanding and his answers.'

Mary and Joseph were also astonished. In reply to Mary's question about his parents' 'anxiously searching' for him Jesus replied, 'Didn't you know I had to be in my Father's house?' (Luke 2:49).

Jewish elders.

Jesus and the money-changers

Jesus referred once more to the Temple as his 'Father's house' (see John 2:12-17). He went to the Temple and found the Court of the Gentiles full of traders and money-changers, making huge profits as they exchanged Jewish coins for 'pagan' currency.

21 days before the Passover the priests began to collect the Temple tax, which had to be paid annually by every Israelite, whether rich or poor. The tax was supposed to atone for the donor's sins and contributed to the Temple running and maintenance expenses (Exodus 30:11-18).

Had the traders been confined to the streets around the Temple, all would have been well. The *Talmud* records that a certain Babha Ben Buta had been the first to introduce '3,000 sheep of the flocks of Kedar' into the Court of the Gentiles. His profane example was eagerly followed, until in Jesus' day the stench and filth of flocks of penned sheep and oxen filled the air as they were bargained for by the traders and visiting pilgrims.

Jesus made a whip of cords and drove them all, including the cattle and sheep, from the Temple area. To those who sold doves he said, 'Get these out of here! How dare you turn my Father's house into a market!'

Jesus denounced Jewish leaders who paraded themselves on street corners, wearing extra-long tassels on their prayer shawls and displaying their extra-wide phylacteries (Matthew 23:1-5).

Many Jews wore phylacteries on their wrists and foreheads, in literal obedience to God's command to 'tie his instructions on their hands and foreheads' (Deuteronomy 6:8). The tiny boxes contained parchments with hand-written extracts from the Old Testament law on them.

Jesus and the Festivals

Probably every year Jesus visited the Temple for the three great feasts of Passover, Pentecost and Tabernacles, when every able-bodied man in Israel was commanded by the Law of Moses to present himself before the Lord in Jerusalem (Deuteronomy 16:16).

Jesus often seized these opportunities, when vast crowds were gathered in the Temple courts, to teach the people about the kingdom of God and the purpose of his ministry (Luke 19:47; 20:21). It is reckoned that the four Gospel writers mention Jesus visiting the Temple on 14 separate occasions.

The Religious Leaders

Some of Jesus' sharpest encounters with the leading religious authorities in Jerusalem took place in the Temple courts.

On one occasion, the chief priests and the Pharisees sent the Temple guards to arrest Jesus as he was teaching in the Temple courts. When they heard Christ's teaching, they were spellbound. On returning to the chief priests and Pharisees, the guards were asked, 'Why didn't you bring him in?' 'No-one ever spoke the way this man does,' they declared (John 7:32-52).

The Temple Destroyed

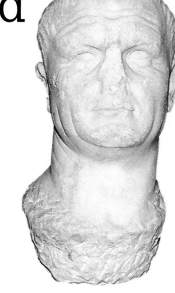

In AD 66 the Jews rebelled against their Roman masters. Herod's Temple became the focal point of resistance, from where the Jews held out against the might of Rome. By August of AD 70 all of Jerusalem except the Temple was in Roman hands.

Since the Temple was one of the wonders of the ancient world, the Romans hesitated before destroying it. But the stubborn zealots refused to surrender, even though they stood no chance against the overwhelming numbers, war-machines, armaments and discipline of the world's best army.

The Romans, under Titus, responded by torching the Temple, setting fire to all its woodwork, and even throwing a lighted torch into the sanctuary itself. Before the building was reduced to a heap of rubble the Romans grabbed some of its priceless furnishings, thinking what excellent trophies they would make for their victory parade back in Rome.

In literal fulfilment of Jesus' prophecy that 'not one stone here will be left on another; every one will be thrown down' (Matthew 24:2), all that remained of Herod's Temple by the time the Roman army had finished was the platform on which it was built.

The massacre

The Romans were always ruthlessly efficient in warfare. In crushing the resistance of the Jewish zealots, the Romans massacred all the inhabitants who had failed to flee to the

The Emperor Vespasian AD 69-79.

surrounding mountains. From the time that Titus had laid siege to the city to the time the last stone of the Temple was pulled down it is estimated that more than one million Jews were slaughtered.

The Titus Arch, Rome, built to commemorate Titus' victory over the Jews.

The Temple Plundered

Rome was no friend to the early Christians. Under Nero, the emperor who preceded Vespasian, the Christians had been persecuted and blamed for its great fire, and the apostle Paul martyred.

Rome was proud of her military victories. A commemorative arch, the Titus Arch, was built in Rome and showed soldiers carrying off the priceless treasures they had plundered from the Jerusalem Temple in AD 70.

The relief below shows the Romans triumphantly carrying the seven-branched golden lampstand. This is the only contemporary depiction of furniture from the Temple extant today.

Titus, the successful Roman commander, who crushed the Jews and destroyed their Temple in AD 70.

A hoard of silver shekels, dating from AD 66-70, with the oil lamp with which they were discovered by archaeologists. They were probably hidden by a frightened Jewish family during the Roman assault on Jerusalem in AD 70.

After 3,000 Years . . .

Since the destruction of the Temple in AD 70, the holiest shrine in the Jewish world is the western side of the wall that Herod the Great built to enclose his Temple area. It is the only remaining link with the Temple.

Many of the stone blocks in this wall date from Herod's time, and average 1.2 metres (4 feet) high and from 1 to 7 metres (4 to 24 feet) long. Before the Arab-Israeli partition of Jerusalem in 1948, and since the Six Days War of 1967, Jews have prayed at the Western Wall. Jews, many in traditional dress, observe the Sabbath here each week

A Jewish boy celebrates his barmitzvah, reading from the Torah scroll, at the Western Wall in Jerusalem.

The Wailing Wall

The wall has also been called the Wailing Wall, or Wall of Lamentation. The Jews gather here to mourn the loss of their Temple, replicating a similar experience recorded by the Book of Lamentations, over the earlier destruction of Jerusalem and Solomon's Temple: 'How deserted lies the city, once so full of people! . . . This is why I weep and my eyes overflow with tears. . . . The Lord has rejected his altar and abandoned his sanctuary' (Lamentations 1:1, 16; 2:7). There is even a tradition that the drops of dew which form on the stones are tears shed by the wall in sympathy with the exiled Jews!

For religious Jews, the destruction of Jerusalem was an unmitigated disaster, as the whole sacrificial system was terminated. But Christians realised that the Temple had served its purpose. The very first thing that Matthew records in his Gospel, after Jesus' death, is that 'the curtain of the temple [the "veil" which sectioned off the Holiest Place from the Holy Place] was torn in two from top to bottom' (Matthew 27:51). Jesus had opened up God's presence to us (see also Hebrews 6:19-20; 10:19-22).

Orthodox Jews pray at the
Western Wall.

The Temple Mount from the Air

The original Temple site is traced back to Mount Moriah, where Abraham, who lived about 1,000 years before David, built an altar to offer up his son Isaac in obedience to God's command (Genesis 22).

This is the same mountaintop that David chose as the site on which the Temple should stand. David bought from Araunah his threshing floor and the surrounding area, because it was where David confessed his sin of numbering the people and where the plague was stayed. David paid Araunah 600 shekels of gold and declared, 'Here shall be the house of the Lord God and here the altar of burnt offering for Israel' (see 1 Chronicles 21-22).

Solomon's Temple, Herod's Temple and now the Dome of the Rock all claim to have been built on this exact location.

A Heavenly Temple

The destruction of Jerusalem and its Temple by the Romans is nowhere mentioned in the New Testament, even though some of the New Testament books were penned after AD 70. Most of the early Christians were converts from Judaism; how did they cope without the Temple?

A spiritual temple

The writer of the letter to the Hebrews does not describe the Temple building (as the Old Testament books do in some detail), but explains the Temple's spiritual significance. Hebrews directs the reader's attention to the heavenly temple, using the earthly temple to illustrate Christian teaching, now that the crucified and risen Christ is in heaven.

▪ Solomon's Temple was only 'a copy and shadow' of the heavenly temple (Exodus 25:8-9; Hebrews 8:5).

▪ The true holy place is the heavenly one (Hebrews 9:24).

▪ The heavenly sanctuary belongs to the new covenant (Hebrews 6:19-20).

▪ Because Christ is our high priest, and already in the heavenly temple, Christians take part in its worship now (Hebrews 10:19-25).

▪ The heavenly temple is 'the church of the firstborn [i.e. Christians], whose names are written in heaven' (Hebrews 12:23).

▪ Paul also writes that Christians are God's 'holy temple' (Ephesians 2:19-22), and Peter that Christians are 'stones' in the temple building (1 Peter 2:5).

The new Jerusalem

The book of Revelation, echoing Isaiah's vision and Ezekiel's vision, visualises the new heavenly Jerusalem as 'the Holy City, the new Jerusalem, coming down out of heaven from God, prepared as a bride beautifully dressed for her husband. And I heard a loud voice from the throne saying, "Now the dwelling of God is with men, and he will live with them. They will be his people, and God himself will be with them and be their God' (Revelation 21:2-3).

The Temple Mount viewed through the window of the Chapel of Dominus Flevit on the Mount of Olives.

No temple in heaven

Surely something is missing. Isn't the statement 'I did not see a temple in the city' (Revelation 21:22) the ultimate anti-climax? No temple in heaven? After the Tabernacle, Solomon's Temple and Herod's Temple there is now no temple!

The Western Wall of the Temple Mount viewed from near the Dung Gate.

What may seem disappointing proves to be the opposite, for John completes his sentence, 'I did not see a temple in the city' with the words, 'because the Lord the Almighty and the Lamb are its temple'. The 'loud voice' (Revelation 21:3) had already declared, 'Now the dwelling of God is with men, and he will live with them.'

When Moses spoke with God in the Tabernacle 'as with a friend', he was experiencing heaven on earth – the whole point of the Temple. In heaven no temple is necessary because 'the Lord Almighty and the Lamb are its temple'.

The Golden Gate, Jerusalem, through which, tradition has it, Jesus will return.

Index

Acknowledgments

Illustrations
James Macdonald: p. 13
Alan Parry: pp. 4-5, 6-7, 14, 23
Paul Wyart: pp. 10-11

Photographs
CMJ: pp.3, 21, 22
Three's Company/Tiger Colour Library: pp. 8, 12 (bottom), 24, 25 (top and right), 26, 27, 30-31
Zev Radovan: pp.12 (top), 25 (bottom left), 28-29
Alec Garrard (Temple Model): pp.1, 9, 13, 15, 16-17, 18-19, 20